LILY BLOOM'S

THIS JOURNAL BELONGS TO:

MW00608494